W9-CUG-827

Keep the kettle boiling

Keep the kettle boiling

Rhymes from a Belfast childhood

Maggi Kerr Peirce

Illustrated by
Barbara Allen

Appletree Press

First published and printed by
The Appletree Press Ltd
7 James Street South
Belfast BT2 8DL
1983

10 9 8 7 6 5 4 3 2 1

British Library Cataloguing in Publication Data
Peirce, Maggi Kerr
  Keep the kettle boiling: rhymes from a Belfast
childhood.
  1. Children's songs, Irish
  I. Title   II. Allen, Barbara
  398'.8   GR475

ISBN 0-86281-116-3

To Morrel, Derek, Jack and Dorothy,
this book is lovingly dedicated

Maggi Kerr Peirce was born in Belfast
in 1931 and has lived in Stockholm,
Amsterdam, London and Edinburgh, where she was a
founding member of the Edinburgh University Folksong
Society. She gives regular public readings of her stories,
and in 1982 a cassette of her work was issued by Yellow
Moon Press, Cambridge, Mass. Since 1964 she has lived in
the United States, where whe is married with twin
children. She teaches at Roger Williams College in Rhode
Island.

Barbara Allen was born in 1959 in Belfast, where she still
lives. She was educated at Glengormley High School, and
in 1982 graduated from the Ulster Polytechnic, Art and
Design Centre, where she is currently doing postgraduate
work.

Contents

Introduction

In compiling this collection of street and schoolyard gleanings from my childhood in Belfast, I have been faced with the unenviable task of asking myself why these rhymes have stayed with me all these years. Was my childhood 'the rosy hours' so vividly described in story and song?

Alas, how far this is from the truth. My early days were fraught with peril, hurt feelings, and rough sobs under the blankets. Yet, somehow, there was something magical about those years, and the chants and taunts that I have set down in the following pages were part and parcel of that tremulous period. They flowed around me in the streets, charmed me in the playground, and enchanted and wove a spell about me that I have never been able to quite shake off.

It seems only yesterday that I was running down Irwin Avenue, on the east side of Belfast, bobbed hair bouncing wildly, scab-encrusted knees twinkling madly, mouthing 'wee rhymes' as I went.

I was born in 1931 in the city of Belfast. My father was a policeman, my mother a housewife, who warbled as she polished the taps and told me stories. I had one sister, Dorothy, a multitude of first cousins, who were as close as brothers and sisters to me, and all my aunts, on both sides of my family, were my second mothers.

In Belfast, I was a pupil at Strandtown Public Elementary School. During the war, I spent several months in Killinchy, Co. Down, attending the two-roomed school on the hill, but except for a further six months of Business School at Mercantile, near Clifton Street, this was the extent of my education. At the age of fourteen and a half, I was hurled to the lions of big business in Belfast.

There seemed no time for truly growing or maturing. It was all brash, harsh and perplexing to me… but interesting. So I 'put away my childish things', and among those were all the rhymes I'd learned in the streets, giggled in draughty corridors, or skipped to, with the rope sounding 'thwack! thwack!' on the pavement.

Finally, I wrote down all of the taunts, chants and wee songs that I could recall, and the reason for doing this, was really very simple. There is something very comforting about remembering your beginnings, when love was only an arm's length away in the kitchen, and life was small and cosy, and all your relatives were endearing or funny, or both. Of course, variations of these rhymes are known not only in other places, but also in Belfast itself. I have simply recorded here those versions that I myself knew as a child.

I hope you will like what I have remembered, that you will have a good giggle and, if you are older, that it may stir some happy memories for you too.

Maggi Kerr Peirce
Fairhaven,
Mass.

1 Rhymes for babies

In our family we had twenty-one first cousins and we all mixed freely as most of us lived within easy walking distance of one another. As almost all the women on both sides of the family became pregnant at the same time, I don't remember too many babies but the few that we had were always sung, dandled and bounced to various songs and rhymes. Happy, dribbling little faces, with hiccups, are my memory of fond grown-ups swinging wee mites high in the air, their arms and faces full of love and laughter.

15

Rub a dub dub
Three men in a tub,
The Butcher, the Baker
The Candlestick maker,
All jumped into a rotten potato;
With a high... swing
And a low... swing
And a wee one into the bar–gain.

Round and round the garden
Like a little mouse
One jump, two jump
And into the little house.

18

See, saw,
Marjorie Daw
Sold her wee bed
To lie upon straw.

Wasn't she a dirty slut
To sell her bed
And lie in muck?

Round and round the garden
Like a teddy bear
One step, two step
And tickle you under there.

Here's the church
And here's the steeple
Open the door
And here's the people.

Clap hands for daddy-o
My bonny wee babby-o
You'll get fish
In your wee dish
Butter on your bread
When your daddy comes home.

Dance to your daddy, my bonny laddy—
Dance to your daddy, to your mammy sing.
You'll get a fishy, in a little dishy—
You'll get a fishy, when the boat comes home.

Knock the knocker (*forehead*)
Peep in (*eyes*)
Lift the latch (*nose*)
Walk in (*mouth*).

These are the lady's knives and forks
Here's the lady's table
This is the lady's looking glass
And here's the baby's cradle.

Creepy, creepy, little mouse
All the way to 'Henry's' house.

Put your finger in the crow's nest,
She's not at home,
She's away to Ballybannon
To get a marrow bone.

She's coming, she's coming
She's at the very gate
(she grabs the finger):

2 Skipping songs and rhymes

Skipping ropes for the girls and hoops for the boys came out of cupboards in springtime. When I was growing up hoops were going out of fashion, but I can still hear the dinging sound of a hoop being bowled along the pavement and see, in the mind's eye, all the different forms of hopscotch scrawled with huge hunks of rock chalk up and down Lomond Avenue with little girls, like storks, tongues gripped in concentration between teeth, hopping madly from square to square.

Skipping was always a lot of fun—I think I was a pretty good skipper but no more than another score of girls in the neighbourhood. It was almost like gaining girlhood from childhood to be able to do all the different rhymes properly, with actions, and not to be lashed by the rope. Many an aching leg I took home in the evening for if the rope were at all wet, a viciously pulled rope (and those kind of children were around then too) could give you a welt on your leg which would not die away for a good two weeks.

Keep the kettle boiling,
Miss the rope you're out,
If you had a been
Where I had a been,
You wouldn't ha' been put out.

A very good morning to you, sir,
Where have you been, sir?
Been to the North Pole, sir,
What were you doing there, sir?
Catching polar bears, sir,
How many did you catch, sir?
One, sir, two, sir (*etc.*).

My gypsy lady,
Won't you be my baby?
I know I love you
I know I do.
For in the springtime
The pretty ringtime
I know I love you
You know I do.

All together girls,
This fine weather girls;
I spied a lark,
Sitting in the dark;
L–O, L–O,
G–O, GO!

Vote, vote, vote for (Margaret Beatty),
In comes (Chatty) at the door;
Now (Chatty) is the one
Who will have a bit of fun
So we don't want (Margaret) anymore.

Vote, vote, vote for (Chatty Kelly),
In comes (Dorothy) at the door;
For (Dorothy) is the one
Who will have a bit of fun
And we don't want (Chatty) anymore.

*(The names in brackets were those of people we
knew, and can be replaced with names of your
choice).*

Ducky Ducky do,
It's half past two,
Swimming on the water
With a wee black shoe.

I know a lady
Her name is Miss;
And all of a sudden
She went like THIS (*straddle on 'this'*)

Ingle angle, silver bangle,
Ingle angle out—
If you ha' been
Where I ha' been
You wouldn't ha' been out.

On the mountain stands a lady,
Who she is I do not know.
All she wants is gold and silver,
All she wants is a nice young man.
Lady, lady, touch the ground,
Lady, lady, turn right round;
Lady, lady, show your shoe,
Lady, lady, run right through.

Polly in the kitchen,
Doin' a bit of stitchin',
In comes a bogey man
And out goes she.

Jelly on a plate,
Jelly on a plate,
Wibble, wobble,
Wibble, wobble,
Jelly on a plate.

Paddy on the railroad
Picking up stones,
Down comes an engine
And breaks Paddy's bones;
'Ouch' says Paddy,
'That's not fair!'
'Ouch!' say the engine,
'I don't care.'

Cowboy Joe, from Mexico,
Hands up,
Stick 'em up,
And out you go!

I am a girlguide dressed in blue,
These are the actions I can do:
Stand at ease,
Bend your knees,
Salute to the King,
Bow to the Queen,
Quick march through the arch,
One, two, three… (*fast*)

Would you like to play a game?
Try and guess this boy's name.
It starts with G,
It ends with E.
Come and skip and play with me.

On the mountain stands a school
And in that school there is a desk
And on that desk there is a book
And in that book there is my name.
Ten boy's names must I know;
Wish me luck for here I go:
David, Billy, John, Robert,
Paul, Mark, Peter,
Gordon, Kenneth, Joe.

Two little sausages
Frying in the pan,
One got burnt
And the other said,
'Scram!'

Teddy Bear, Teddy Bear,
Go upstairs,
Teddy Bear, Teddy Bear,
Say your prayers,
Teddy Bear, Teddy Bear,
Switch out the light,
Teddy Bear, Teddy Bear,
Say good-night.

(*first version*)

Teddy Bear, Teddy Bear,
Turn right around,
Teddy Bear, Teddy Bear,
Touch the ground,
Teddy Bear, Teddy Bear,
Show your shoe,
Teddy Bear, Teddy Bear,
Run right through.

(*second version*)

Strawberry, apple, blackberry tart,
Tell me the name of your sweetheart,
A, B, C, D (*etc.*)

Cinderella
Dressed in yella
Went upstairs to see her fella.
How many kisses did she get?
One, two, three, four (*etc.*)

Apple jelly, black currant jam,
Tell me the name of your young man.
A, B, C, D (*etc.*)

I love coffee, I love tea,
I love the girls and the girls love me.
I wish my mother would hold her tongue,
For she had a boy when she was young.

I had a dress and it was green,
I didn't like it so I gave it to the queen,
The queen didn't like it so she gave it to the king,
Shut your eyes, and count sixteen.

Father, father, may I go
Away to the London Ball?
Yes, my daughter, you may go
Away to the London Ball.
Button up our coats and away we'll go,
Away to the London Ball.

Granny, Granny, I am sick,
Send for the doctor, quick, quick, quick.

I had a little shoe and it was blue,
It died last night at a quarter past two,
I put it in a coffin,
It fell through the bottom,
My little shoe, dressed in blue.

Two little dickie birds sittin' on a wall,
One called Peter and the other called Paul;
Fly away Peter, fly away Paul,
Come back Peter, come back Paul.

Gather in, gather in,
For a big, big, ring;
If you don't come quick
You won't get in.

Bluebells, cockle shells,
Evy, ivy, overhead.
My mammy does the washing,
My daddy cuts the meat,
How many hours
Does the baby sleep?
One, two, three, four (*etc.*)

I'll tell me ma, when I go home,
The boys won't leave the girls alone,
They tossed my hair, they broke my comb,
But that's all right till I get home.
She is handsome, she is pretty,
She is the belle of Belfast City;
She is courting, one, two, three,
Please can you tell me who is he?
Albert Mooney says he loves her,
All the boys are fighting for her,
They knock at the door and they ring at the bell,
Saying, 'Oh, my true love, are you well?'
Out she comes, as white as snow,
With rings on her fingers
And bells on her toes,
Oul' Jenny Murray says she'll die
If she doesn't get the fella with a roving eye.
Let the rain and the wind and the breeze blow high
The snow comes falling from the sky,
Jenny Murray says she'll die
If she doesn't get the fella with a roving eye.
One young man is fighting for her,
All the rest they swear they'll have her,
Let them all say as they will,
Albert Mooney loves her still.

I had a little bubble car in 1968,
I took it round the corner and slammed on the
   brakes.
The policeman caught me and took me to jail.
How many years was I in jail?
One, two, three, four (*etc.*)

I love coffee,
I love tea,
I love the boys
And the boys love me.

House to let,
Apply within,
A lady put out
For drinking gin.

Big Ben
Strikes ten
In the middle of London,
One, two, three, four (*etc.*)

I come from Chinky China,
From Chinky China Sea;
I wash my clothes in Dinah,
For fifty shillings a week—OUT!

Ala Bala Busha, the King of the Jews,
Bought his wife a new pair of shoes.
When the shoes began to wear
Ala Bala Busha began to swear:
Lady, lady, touch the ground,
Lady, lady, turn right around;
Lady, lady, show your shoe,
Lady, lady, run right through.

3 Rhymes for other games

The world nowadays always seems to pity the city dweller, but I think that one can have the most wonderful love affairs with cities—tender and loving and knowing. And though Belfast may not be the most beautiful city in the world, I grew up in it with my eyes forever sweeping the skyline where the hills were—for Belfast was surrounded by mountains, hills and glens as far as the eye could see, and even in the worst quarters of the inner city one could always see the misty blueness of shadow or the wide swirling sweep of mist over the tops of the fair setting which houses the industrial squalor which is Belfast.

I lived two miles from the city centre. It was the usual case of lower middle-class morality with its livid gossip, bigoted outlook and simpering respectability subsisting, terrace house by terrace house, in the noisy exuberance of the lower Newtownards Road with its row houses, paper-boats-in-the-gutter, women with curlers like corkscrews and arms akimbo holding up their front doors as they watched life go by. I did not care for the children who lived in the rarified air of my home street and, praise be to God, had a mother who never said 'No' when I scampered off to the less ethereal heights to play ball, have wee concerts in back entries (skinny legs and thick red ribbons in silver tapdance shoes) and skip to my heart's content with the big rope going 'thwack, thwack' against the cement.

Ball-game rhymes

One, two, three, O'Leary,
Four, five, six, O'Leary,
Seven, eight, nine, O'Leary,
Ten, O'Leary – O.

One, two, three, O'Leary,
I saw Mrs O'Leary
Sitting on her bumba-leery
Eatin' could pease porridge.

Plainy, clappy, roly-poly,
Ding, dong dushy, touch the ground,
Burl a round.

Desperate Dan, thinks he's grand,
But he can't do upsie;
Desperate Dan, thinks he's grand,
But he can't do dropsie;
Desperate Dan, thinks he's grand,
But he can't do dizzie;
Desperate Dan, thinks he's grand,
But he can't do pipsie;
Desperate Dan, thinks he's grand,
But he can't do bouncie.

Bounce ball, bounce ball,
One, two, three;
Underneath my right leg
And round about my knee;
Bounce ball, bounce ball,
Bird or bee,
Flying from the rosebud
Up into a tree.

Bounce ball, bounce ball,
Fast you go,
Underneath my left leg
And round about my toe;
Bounce ball, bounce ball,
Butt – er – fly,
Flying from the rosebud
Up into the sky.

Queenie, queenie,
Who's got the ball?
I haven't got it,
I haven't got it,
I haven't got it,
In my pocket.

Game, game, ba', ba',
Twenty lassies in a row,
Not a boy among them a'.

Upsie Mother Brown,
Upsie Mother Brown,
Upsie, upsie,
Double times upsie,
Upsie Mother Brown.

Dropsie Mother Brown,
Dropsie Mother Brown,
Dropsie, dropsie,
Double times dropsie,
Dropsie Mother Brown.

Dixie Mother Brown,
Dixie Mother Brown,
Dixie, dixie,
Double times dixie,
Dixie Mother Brown.

Games—inside and outside

In and out the dusty bluebells,
In and out the dusty bluebells,
In and out of the dusty bluebells,
I love my Master.

Tipper-ipper-apper on her left shoulder,
Tipper-ipper-apper on her left shoulder,
Tipper-ipper-apper on her left shoulder,
I love my Master.

The Grand Old Duke of York,
He had so many men,
He marched them up to the top of the hill
And he marched them down again.
And when they were up, they were up,
And when they were down they were down,
And when they were only half way up,
They were neither up nor down.

Here we go lubby-lu,
Here we go lubby-li,
Here we go lubby-lu,
All on a Saturday night-ho!

Put your right hand in,
Put your right hand out,
Shake it a little, a little,
And turn yourself about-ho!

The cows are in the meadow,
Laying down to rest,
Around the king, around the queen,
We all jump up together again.

The farmer wants a wife,
The farmer wants a wife,
Ay-o, me neery-o,
The farmer wants a wife.

The wife wants a child,
The wife wants a child,
Ay-o, me neery-o,
The wife wants a child.

The child wants a dog,
The child wants a dog,
Ay-o, me neery-o,
The child wants a dog.

The dog wants a bone,
The dog wants a bone,
Ay-o, me neery-o,
The dog wants a bone.

Ha ha, look at the bone,
Ha ha, look at the bone,
Ay-o, me neery-o,
Ha ha, look at the bone.

(everyone thumps the unfortunate bone)

Down on the carpet, we shall kneel,
While the grass grows round our feet,
Stand up straight upon your feet,
And choose the one you love so sweet.

Now they're married, life and joy,
First a girl and then a boy,
Seven years after, seven years to come,
Oh, Geordie, Geordie, kiss and run.
Oh, Geordie, Geordie, have another one.

Paddy from Cork has never been,
Never a railway train has seen,
Never seen the great machine,
That travels along the railroad.

London Bridge is falling down,
Falling down, falling down,
London Bridge is falling down,
My fair lady.

What will we do with London Bridge,
London Bridge, London Bridge,
My fair lady?

Buckle it up with iron bars,
Iron bars, iron bars,
Buckle it up with iron bars,
And then it will never be broken.
(arch made by first couple)

We are the robbers coming through,
Coming through, coming through,
We are the robbers coming through,
My fair lady.

What did the robbers do to you,
Do to you, do to you,
What did the robbers do to you,
My fair lady?

They stole my watch and stole my chain,
Stole my chain, stole my chain,
They stole my watch and stole my chain,
My fair lady.

(This is an arch game, where the victim is caught in the arch and then asked to take his or her choice of silver or gold. Eventually two teams are made up of the 'silver' and the 'gold' selectors, who have a tug-of-war.)

Hurly, burly, trumpet tray,
The cow shit in the market,
Some go far, and some go near,
Where does this poor Frenchman steer?

Grandma, Grandma Grey,
Will you let us out to play,
We won't go near the water
To chase the ducks away.

Go along with you childer.
(she chases them)

In and out the windows,
In and out the windows,
In and out the windows,
As you have done before.

Stand and face your partner,
Stand and face your partner,
Stand and face your partner,
As you have done before.

A penny for a cotton spool,
A penny for a needle,
That's the way the money goes,
Pop! goes the weasle.

Half a pound of twopenny rice,
Half a pound of treacle,
That's the way the money goes,
Pop! goes the weasle.

Numerical or choosing rhymes

Pig
Snout
Walk
Out!

Magpies seen:

One for sorrow,
Two for joy,
Three for a kiss,
Four for a boy,
Five for silver,
Six for gold,
Seven for a secret never to be told,
Eight for a letter from across the sea,
Nine for a lover as true as can be.

One, two, three,
My mother caught a flea,
She roasted it, she toasted it,
We had it for our tea.

One, two, three, four,
Mary at the cottage door,
Eating plums off a plate,
Five, six, seven, eight.

One potato, two potato, three potato, four
Five potato, six potato, seven potato, MORE!

One, two, three, four, five, six, seven,
All good children go to heaven,
When they die, their sins forgiven,
One, two, three, four, five, six, seven.

Zeentie, teentie, figgerie fell,
Ell dell dromonell,
Arkie, parkie, terrie rope,
Zam, tam, toozie joke,
You are OUT!

One, two, buckle my shoe,
Three, four, knock at the door,
Five, six, cut up sticks,
Seven, eight, lay them straight,
Nine, ten, the big fat hen.

One, two, three, four, five,
Once I caught a fish alive.
Why did you let it go?
Because it bit my finger so.
Which finger did it bite?
This little finger on the right.

4 School rhymes

Canes were used throughout our school, until I was ten years of age when we suddenly were told by the new headmaster that girls were no longer to be caned, only reprimanded. Most of the teachers had their canes hanging on the outside of their cupboards and the slap was always given on the palm of the hand. If the cane were badly frayed at the end, it gave a really severe cut, but we all preferred this to a rap over the knuckles with a pointer or a glancing blow from our sewing mistress, whose temper and large rings were legend in the annals of school history.

Are you HUNGARY,
Yes SIAM,
RUSSIA to the table,
And I'll FIJI,
Some TURKEY.

GERMANY was HUNGARY,
Took a bit of TURKEY,
Dipped it into GREECE,
And fried it in JAPAN.

Taffy was a Welshman;
Taffy was a thief;
Taffy came to our house
And stole a lump of beef.

Tell tale tit,
Your tongue shall be slit,
And all the doggies in the town
Shall have a little bit.

Dublin on the Liffey
Yorkshire on the Ooze
Belfast on the Lagan
And McMordie on the booze.

(McMordie was our headmaster.)

England, Ireland, Scotland, Wales,
All tied up with donkeys' tails.

Cur – i – osity killed the cat,
Information made him fat.

Our wee school is a nice wee school,
It's made with bricks and mortar,
And the only thing that's wrong with it
Is the baldy-headed master.

If you weren't so Ballymena
With your Ballymoney,
You could have a Ballycastle
For your Ballyholme.

The boy stood on the burning deck,
The captain sounded the hooter,
And what do you think came sailing by
But Hitler on his scooter.

Give a thing.
Take a thing.
The bad man's gold ring.

You can walk on a shamrock;
You can eat a leak;
You can pluck a rose;
But you can't sit on a thistle.

*After midday on April Fool's Day no further
fooling is accepted and if it is tried, this is what
is taunted:*

April Fool is dead and gone,
You're the fool for carrying on.
Three potatoes in a pot
You're the fool
And I am NOT!

5 Street rhymes

We always walked to school, arms twined round waists and whispering secrets with schoolbags of leather bouncing against rounded rumps. It was about a mile walk from home and we never went the same way on our return. We would trip along the ringing pavements in summer (always missing the black cracks or you'd marry a 'nigger', though none of us at that time had even seen a person with black skin) or splash along the puddle-peppered streets in winter, giving vent to our songs to hurry us home to tea of golden cutlets and chips.

Snug
As a bug
In a rug.

Camphor Balls
Four-a-penny,
If you don't come quick
You won't get any.

I know who is sick
I know who is sorry
I know who I've kissed
But God knows who I'll marry.

Mammy, I'm on the shelf.
What are you doin', ye divil ye?
Mammy, I'm breaking the delft.
Tear away, ye divil ye.

Skinnymalink, melodeon legs,
Big banana feet,
Went to the pictures
And couldn't get a seat;
When he got a seat
He fell fast asleep,
Skinnymalink, melodeon legs,
Big banana feet.

Our wee queen can birl her leg,
Birl her leg, birl her leg,
Our wee queen can birl her leg,
Birl–her–leg.

Our wee queen can tumble her pole,
Tumble her pole, tumble her pole,
Our wee queen can tumble her pole,
Tumble–her–pole.

Our queen's up the river
With a fa-la-la,
Our queen's up the river
With a fa-la-la,
Our queen's up the river
And we'll keep her there forever,
With a fa-la-la-la.

Over the garden wall
I let the baby fall
M' mother came out
And gave me a clout
Over the garden wall.

(first version)

Over the garden wall
I let the baby fall
M' mother came out
And turned m' bloomers inside out.

(second version)

Old mother witch
Fell in a ditch
Found a penny
And thought she was rich.

Our queen won
The other had to run,
Hi ho m' deery–o
Our queen won.

Cowmaneery, kilt me keery
Cowmaneery–neery
Pins stone stra-ma-diddle
Narry a bone-a-ring-ting-ning
Dum a bull-a-coi me.

My can was new my can was new,
I only had it a day or two.
I'll punch a hole in your can
For punching a hole in my can.

Sally Walker sells fish,
Three ha'pence a dish,
Cut their heads off,
Cut their tails off,
Sally Walker sells fish.

Look up
Look down
You owe me
Half-a-crown.

Good night
Sleep tight
Don't let the bugs bite.

And if they bite
Hold them tight,
They'll not come back
Another night.

I beg your pardon
I grant your grace
I hope the cat
Will spit in your face.

Oh my finger
Oh my thumb
Oh my belly
And my rum-a-tum-tum.

Ochenee,
The poor banshee,
Many's a shift
It's made for me.

Sally go round the stars
Sally go round the moon
Sally go round the chimney pots
On a Saturday afternoon.

Adam and Eve went up my sleeve
And didn't come down
To Hallow's Eve.

I went to a river
I couldn't get across,
I paid five shillings
For an old jackass;
I jumped on its back
And its bones gave a crack,
Now who'll play the fiddle
Till I come back?

Hi for Saturday night,
Sunday's long a-coming,
And I'm going down the town
For to see my sweetheart coming.

He wears a little topcoat
And his waistcoat's in the fashion,
But he has to lie in bed
While his Sunday's shirt's awashing.

Such is life in all its phases,
When you die you go to blazes!

God bless my soul,
Would you buy a wooden bowl,
And suck coul' porridge
In the mornin'?

This is the boy that broke into the barn
This is the boy that stole the corn
This is the boy that bent the saw
And this is the boy that told all
And poor Willie Winkie had to pay for it all.

Dan, Dan, the funny wee man,
Washed his face in the frying pan,
Combed his hair with a donkey's tail,
And scratched his belly with his big toenail.

There was a crooked man
Who walked a crooked mile,
He found a crooked sixpence
Beside a crooked style,
He bought a crooked cat
Who caught a crooked mouse
And they all lived together
In a little crooked house.

A whistling maid
Or a crowing hen
Were neither made
For God nor men.

I wish I were a furry worm
And had a furry tummy
I'd walk across a lollypop
And make my tummy
Gummy!

Boys a dear, I found a penny,
Boys a dear, I bought a bap,
Boys a dear, I ate it up,
Boys a dear, it made me fat.

Let's go to bed, says Sleepy-head,
Let's wait awhile, says Slow,
Put on the pot, says Greedy Guts,
An' we'll ate before we go.

Ochenee, when I was wee
I used to sit on my granny's knee;
Her apron tore,
I fell on the floor,
Ochenee, when I was wee.

Sticks and stones may break my bones
But names will never hurt me,
And when I'm dead and in my grave
You'll suffer what you called me.

There was an old man called Michael Finnegan,
He grew whiskers on his chinnigan,
The wind came up and blew them in again,
Poor old Michael Finnegan-begin-again.

Not last night, but the night before
Three tom cats came knocking at my door,
I went downstairs for to let them in
And they knocked me down with a rolling pin.

Hot cross buns, hot cross buns,
One a penny, two a penny,
Hot cross buns.

If you haven't got a daughter
Give them to your sons,
One a penny, two a penny,
Hot cross buns.

January, February, March,
Stiffen yer whiskers with starch!

Long
Tall
Thin
And
Yella
My
Word
Whata
Fella.

Christmas is coming
And the geese are getting fat,
Please put a penny in the old man's hat.
If you haven't got a penny
A ha'penny will do,
If you haven't got a ha'penny,
God bless you.

O pardon my innocent laugh—Ha, Ha,
Do you know the notes of the staff? Ha, Ha

Tinker, tailor, soldier, sailor,
Rich man, poor man, beggar man, thief,
A royal doctor, a minister, a chief.

*(We recited this rhyme while counting
buttons, to find out who we would marry.)*

Walking rhymes

Left, left,
I had a good job and I left,
I had a good job at fifty bob
And I left, left,
I had a good job and I left.

I wrote a letter to my love
And on the way I dropped it;
Someone must have picked it up
And put it in their pocket.
(This is now used as a rhyme for a ring game.)

Lucy Locket lost her pocket;
Kitty Fisher found it.
There was not a penny in it,
Just a ribbon round it.

Mary Ann Magee,
At half past three
She locked her door
And she turned her key.

(Two people walk with arms crossed; at the word locked *they raise their arms high and bring them down hard; the arms are swivelled round on the word* turned *so that each is walking on a different side from where they started.)*

6 Rude rhymes

On the first day of May our streets blossomed with curtain-bedecked little 'May Queens', usually with a couple of followers. I remember one spring day that I met a group near the school who had walked up from the lower Newtownards Road. The May Queen had a pole with her and when her two pages held it for her, she would hitch up her lace fol-de-rols and, swinging like an agile monkey, she would tumble by feet and clutching hands, round and round.

We stood by, having paid our tuppence for this 'show', filled with admiration and, when she stood on the ground once more, puffing slightly and her face sweating with exertion, we begged her to do it again. 'Only if ye pay me two pennies more,' she demanded. We walked off sadly because, although we lived on the better side of the tracks, we came from homes where appearance was everything and one penny was our pocket-money for a whole week.

She, the May Queen, shrieked, 'Stingy buggers', after us and went proudly off, her small behind bearing, with great dignity, the tattered finery of someone's front parlour.

There was a little man
And he had a little gun,
Over the mountains he did run,
With a little crooked hat
And his belly full of fat
And a pancake stuck to his
Bum, bum, bum.

Do re me fa so la ti do,
What makes me fart?
I do not know.

52 Oh Jo, set me on the po;
I'm not as young as I used to be
Forty years ago.

Our Maggie's blue drawers,
Our Maggie's blue drawers,
There's a hole in the middle
For Maggie to piddle,
Our Maggie's blue drawers.

Mary had a little lamb
She also had a bear;
I've often seen her little lamb
But I've never seen her bear.

There she goes,
There she goes,
All dressed up
In her Sunday clothes;
But nobody knows,
Nobody knows,
Whether she's got
Any underclothes.

(first version)

There she goes,
There she goes,
Stilletto heels
And pointed toes;
Look at her feet,
She thinks she's neat,
Black stockings
And dirty feet.

(second version)

Eenie, meenie, minney, mo,
Catch a nigger by the toe,
When he squeals let him go,
Eenie, meenie, minney, mo.

Eenie, meenie, minney, mo,
Set the baby on the po,
When he's done clean his bum,
Eenie, meenie, minney, mo.

My darlin' Mabel
Swallowed the table
And lost the leg of her drawers.

Come into me arms
Me bundle of charms,
Get out of me sight
You bundle of sh…

Mother, may I go in to swim?
Yes, my darlin' daughter;
Mind the boys don't see yer wee legs,
Keep them under the water.

Down in the valley
Where nobody knows,
There lies Nelly
Without any clothes.

Where e're you be,
Let your wind go free.

God save our Gracious King!
Hit him in the belly with a gravy ring.
God save our King.

Chorus:

Oh dear, what can the matter be?
Three old ladies got locked in the lavatory,
They were there from Monday 'til Saturday,
Nobody knew they were there.

The first ol' lady, Elizabeth Porter,
She was the Bishop of Chichester's daughter,
She went to get rid of some overdue water
And nobody knew she was there.

The second ol' lady, Elizabeth Bender,
She only went there to fix her suspender,
She got it caught up in her feminine gender,
And nobody knew she was there.

The third ol' lady, Elizabeth Humphrey,   53
She sat down and made herself comfy,
She tried to get up but couldn't get her bum
    free,
And nobody knew she was there.

A fourth old lady, Elizabeth Mason,
She couldn't get in so she wet in the basin,
And that is the water I've just washed my face in,
'Cos, I didn't know she'd been there.

Repeat chorus

(Tune: *Johnny's So Long At the Fair*)

Here comes the bride,
Short, fat and wide,
See how she wobbles
From side to side.

(first version)

Here comes the bride,
Sixty inches wide,
See how she wobbles
Her big backside.

(second version)

Shocking, shocking, shocking,
A mouse ran up my stocking.
What did it see when it got to the knee?
Oh, shocking, shocking, shocking!

Tramp, tramp, tramp, the boys are marchin',
Cheer up the bobbies at the door.
If you will not let me in
I will bust yer belly in
And ye'll never see yer daddy anymore.

Irreligious rhymes

Holy Mary, Mother o' God,
Send us down a couple of bob!

Grace:
All people that on earth do dwell,
Grab your forks and eat like hell.

Ashes to ashes
And dust to dust,
If the Lord don't get you
The devil must.

I don't care if it rains or freezes
I am safe in the arms of Jesus,
I am Jesus' little lamb,
Yes, by Jesus Christ I am.

The Salvation Army's free from sin,
All went to heaven in a corned beef tin;
The corned beef tin was made of brass,
They all fell down and skinned their ass.

Andy McClure is a funny wee man,
He goes to church on Sunday;
He prays to God to give him strength,
To bate the kids on Monday.

Political rhymes

Will you come to our wee party, will you come?
Bring your own bread and butter and a bun;
You can bring sugar and tea,
You can come along with me,
Will you come to our wee party, will you come?

(first version)

You're right my boy,
Houl' up yer head,
And be like a gentleman, Sir,
And tell me who King Billy was,
Now tell me if you can, Sir.

Will you come to Abyssinia, will you come?
Bring your own ammunition and a gun;
Mussolini will be there, firing bullets in the air,
Will you come to Abyssinia, will you come?

(second version)

(Tune: *Roll Along, Covered Wagon, Roll Along*)

De Valera had a canary,
Up the leg of his drawers;
It fell down and fell on the ground
And whistled 'The Protestant Boys'.

De Valera had a canary,
Up the leg of his drawers;
He was sleeping and it was peeping
Up the leg of his drawers.

Parodies

Whistle while you work,
Hitler is a squirt,
Goering's barmy,
So's his army,
Rub them all in dirt.

(Tune: *Whistle While You Work*)

John, get up and light the fire,
Turn the gas a wee bit higher,
Go and tell your Aunt Maria,
Baby's got a tooth.

(Tune: *Men of Harlech*)

Does yer pa drink stout?
Does yer mammy know you're out?
Does yer granny wheel the mangle
Round the yard?

That's where the crocodiles chew your legs
And the swans on the river lay hard boiled eggs,
Way down, the Swanee River, no more I'll
    chance to roam
But if my oul' woman had
    the figure like Maud Allen
There'd be no place like home.

(Tune: *Swanee River*)

There is a happy land
Far, far away,
Where we get bread and jam
Three times a day;
Ham and eggs we never see,
Get no sugar in our tea,
You should see us gradually
Fade, fade away.

There is a happy land
Far, far away,
Where we get ham and eggs
Three times a day;
See how the piggies run,
When they see the butcher come,
Three slices off their bum
Three times a day.

There is a happy land
Far, far away,
Where we get bread and jam
Three times a day;
Ham and eggs we never see,
Still we run to the lavatory,
We have bread and jam for tea
Three times a day.

Hark the herald angels sing,
Mrs Simpson stole our king.

Oh, the moon shines so bright
On Charlie Chaplin;
His shoes are cracking
For the want of blacking
And his little baggy trousers
They need mending,
Before we send him
To the Dardenelles.

(Tune: *Pretty Redwing*)

Put me upon an island
Where the girls are few,
Put me among the most
Ferocious lions in the zoo,
Put me upon an island
And I'll never, never fret,
But for pity's sake don't put me
Among the suffragettes.

(Tune: *Spring Song*)

Daisy, Daisy,
What do you think of that;
I upset the cradle
And nearly killed the cat;
The cat began to bubble
So I hit it with the shovel,
It went to bed
With a broken head
And a face like a kangaroo.

(Tune: *Daisy, Daisy*)

I'm Popeye the sailor man,
I come from the Isle of Man;
The seas may be rough
But my muscles are tough,
I'm Popeye the sailor man.

I love to go a-wandering
Down by the chapel door,
And as I go I love to sing
'The Sash My Father Wore'.

(Tune: *I love to Go A-Wandering*)

7 Wee songs and poems

One of my earliest memories is of my father carrying me up the stairs to bed with my feet tucked into the corner of his cardigan as he sang 'I'm the Wee Filoree Man'. Was there ever a safer feeling in the world? Songs, rhymes, gospel hymns, and Harry Lauder songs were common in our household so that, to this day, I can join in the songs of people forty years my senior, and go misty-eyed over the sticky, sentimental tunes of the First World War.

There were rats, rats,
In bowler hats and spats
In the store, in the store.
There were rats, rats,
In bowler hats and spats
In the quartermaster's store.

There were eggs, eggs,
Walking round on legs
In the store, in the store.
There were eggs, eggs,
Walking round on legs
In the quartermaster's store.

There was cheese, cheese,
Walking round on knees
In the store, in the store.
There was cheese, cheese
Walking round on knees
In the quartermaster's store.

There was jelly, jelly,
As fat as Goering's belly
In the store, in the store.
There was jelly, jelly
As fat as Goering's belly
In the quartermaster's store.

62

Someone stole my heart away
Riding on a load of hay,
He looked up and I looked down,
Handsome, sunburnt, Johnny Brown.

Go tell Aunt Susy,
Go tell Aunt Susy,
Go tell Aunt Susy
The old grey goose is dead.

She left five little ducklings,
She left five little ducklings,
She left five little ducklings
To scratch for their own bread.

She died last Sunday,
She died last Sunday,
She died last Sunday
Behind the old grey shed.

Choose, choose, who'll ye tak,
Who'll ye tak, who'll ye tak,
Choose, choose, who'll ye tak,
A lassie or a laddie.

I widnae ha' a laddie-o,
A laddie-o, a laddie-o,
I widnae ha' a laddie-o,
I'd rather hae a lassie.

My da's a millionaire,
Big feet and curly hair;
See him walkin' down the street
With his big banana feet,
My da's a millionaire.

Green Gravel, Green Gravel,
Your grass is so green,
You're the fairest young damsel
That ever I've seen.

Green Gravel, Green Gravel,
Your true lover's dead,
So I've sent you a letter
To turn round your head.

I washed her and I dressed her
And I robed her in silk,
And I wrote down her name with
A glass pen and ink.

(repeat first verse)

Jean was fair
And Jean was fat,
She wore her hair below her hat,
Now what do you think of that?
Fal-de-didle-dide.

Susie Anna, Susie Anna,
Susie made the supper;
She got drunk and the table fell
And she dipped her nose in the butter.

She went to the East and she went to the West
And she went to the Panarama;
But of all the girls that I love best
There's none like Susie Anna.

My Aunt Jane she called me in,
She gave me tea out of her wee tin.
Half a bap with sugar on the top
And three black lumps out of her wee shop.

My Aunt Jane has a bell on the door,
A white stone step and a clean swept floor,
Candy apples, hard green pears,
Conversation lozengers.

My Aunt Jane, she's awful smart,
She bakes wee rings in an apple tart
And when Halloween comes round,
Fornenst that tart I'm always found.

There were three gypsies in a room,
Oh, but they were bonny.
One so sweet, so very, very sweet,
They would charm the heart of a lady-o,
Lady-o, lady-o,
They would charm the heart of a lady-o.

John James O'Hara,
Michael Macnamara,
We're two respected Irishmen
No matter where we go;
We're men of great assurance,
We're noted for our doings,
O'Hara from Tara,
Macnamara from Mayo.

I'm the wee Filoree Man,
A rumplin' tumplin' Tory man,
I'll do all that ever I can
To follow the wee Filoree Man.

Ma ol' da's a workin' man,
He drinks his tea from a wee tin can,
A ha' penny bap and a clipe of ham,
Ma ol' da's a workin' man.

I have a sister, Mary Ann,
She washes her face in a fryin' pan,
Now she's off to hunt for a man,
I have a sister, Mary Ann.

I'm the wee Filoree Man,
A rumplin' tumplin' Tory man,
I'll do all that ever I can
To follow the wee Filoree Man.

Oh, we're marching along,
And we're singing as we go
Of the promised land
Where the beer and whiskey flow.
We are boozers all,
You can tell it by our nose,
We belong to the Salvation Army.

Chorus:
When the beer is on the table,
When the beer is on the table,
When the beer is on the table,
I'll be there!

There was a cow climbed up a tree,
There was a cow climbed up a tree,
There was a cow climbed up a tree,
And you're an awful bum!

Comrades, don't believe him,
Comrades, don't believe him,
Comrades, don't believe him,
As you have done before.

(A song of derision)

The Bangor boat's away,
The Bangor boat's away,
For we won't be home till morning,
We won't be home till morning,
We won't be home till morning,
The Bangor boat's away.

The Bangor boat's away,
We have no time to play,
For we won't be home till morning,
We won't be home till morning,
We won't be home till morning,
The Bangor boat's away.

The Bangor boat's away,
We have no time to stay,
For we won't be home till morning,
We won't be home till morning,
We'll give a wee hush, we'll give a wee push,
The Bangor boat's away.

My dear, do you know, how a long time ago
Two little children whose names I don't know
Were stolen away, one fine summer's day
And left in the woods, so I've heard people say.
Poor babes in the wood, poor babes in the wood,
Oh, won't you remember the babes in the wood.

And when it was night, how sad was their plight,
The sun had gone down and the moon gave no
    light.
They sobbed and they sighed and bitterly cried,
The poor little things, they lay down and died.
Poor babes in the wood, poor babes in the wood,
Oh, won't you remember the babes in the wood.

And when they were dead, the robin so red,
Brought strawberry leaves, and over them spread.
And all the day long, the branches among
Did mournfully whistle and this was their song:
Poor babes in the wood, poor babes in the wood,
Oh, won't you remember the babes in the wood.

I see, said the blind man,
You're a fool, said the dummy,
I'll kick you, said the man with no legs.

If you gently touch a nettle
It will sting you for your pain,
Touch it like a lad of mettle
And it will like silk remain.

'Twas a dark and stormy night
And the rain came down in torrents,
The Bugler's Band sat round the fire
And the captain said to Iona:
'Iona, tell us a tale.'
So, Iona told them a tale,
And the tale went on as follows:
'Twas a dark and stormy night…' (*etc.*)

I have a baby brother,
He's only two months old,
He's such a little darling,
He's worth his weight in gold;
He smiles all day at nothing,
He's a dimple on his cheek,
I'm sure he'd say he loved me,
If only he could speak.

Jolly fine song, jolly well sung,
Jolly fine company, every-one,
If you think you can beat it
You're welcome to try,
But always remember the singer is dry.

Today is my daughter's wedding day,
Ten thousand pounds I'll give away.
(*Cheers of* Good old Squire!)
On second thought, I think it best,
I'll put it in the old oak chest.
(Rotten old Squire!)

When the doctor...
   spectacles on his nose,
Feels your pulse, and says,
   'Well, I suppose
A dose of castor oil is
   the very best thing',
How'd you like to be a baby girl?

When Father Christmas
   brings you lots of toys,
Dolls to cuddle,
   drums to make a noise,
Balls to toss up,
   skipping ropes to twirl,
How'd you like to be a baby girl?

Glorious!
Victorious!
Half a bottle of gin between the four of us,
Thank the Lord there are no more of us.

A very small cat
Had a very large bow,
She thought she looked pretty
So stuck up, you know;
Till one day she stumbled
And forgot all her airs,
For she tripped on her bow
And she fell down the stairs!

Good mornin', Mick,
Good mornin', Pat.
How's yer taties?
Very fat.
How do you ate them?
Skin an' all.
Do you not choke?
Not at all.
Good mornin', Mick,
Good mornin', Pat.

(*first version*)

Good mornin', Mick,
Good mornin', Pat.
Have you been to market?
I have that.
What did you get?
The full o' me hat.
Good mornin', Mick,
Good mornin', Pat.

(*second version*)

The Boers have got my daddy,
My soldier dad;
I don't want to hear my mamma sigh,
I don't want to see my mamma cry;
I'm goin' on a big ship
Across the raging main,
I'm goin' out to fight the Boers I am,
And bring my daddy home again.

I had a little dolly
  and I loved her well.
She had rosy cheeks
  and I called her Rosy Bell.
I taught her how to curtsey
  and how to bow her head
And how to close her sleepy eyes
  when it was time for bed.

I lost my little doll dear,
  as I played on the heath one day.
I cried for a week dear,
  but I never found out where she lay.
Then I found my dear little doll dear,
  as I played on the heath one day.
But she was tattered and torn,
  woebegone and worn
And her beauty all withered away.

We're going to build a house... boo!
A public house... hurrah!
Only one bar... boo!
Forty yards long... hurrah!
No barmen... boo!
Only barmaids... hurrah!
No glasses... boo!
Only buckets... hurrah!
We won't sell beer... boo!
We'll give it away... hurrah!
We'll close at 10 o'clock... boo!
We'll open again at 10:30... hurrah!

A million miles I've travelled,
And a million sights I've seen,
And I'm waiting for the glory seen to be;
But I wonder, yes, I wonder,
Will the angels way up yonder,
Will the angels play their harps for me?

He was only a commoner soldier,
One of the royal recruits,
And he fought for the honour of Hollywood
All for an old pair of boots.
When the baps and buns were flying
He got hit with a hard barmbrack,
But he nobly fell, 'neath the shot and the shell,
Wrapped up in a Union Jack.

A fair little girl sat under a tree,
Sewing as long as her eyes could see;
She smoothed her work and folded it right,
And said, 'Dear work, good night, good night.'
Such a lot of rooks came over her head
Crying, 'Caw, caw,' on their way to bed.
She knew as she watched their curious flight
The dear little things were saying goodnight.
She did not say to the moon goodnight,
She saw him there like a ball of light.
She knew that he had God's work to keep
And over the world could never sleep.